BLOOMS
OF THE
AUSTRALIAN
WILDERNESS

BLOOMS
—OF THE—
AUSTRALIAN
WILDERNESS

PHOTOGRAPHY LEO MEIER

TEXT DENNIS HEARNE

WATTLE
BOOKS

A KEVIN WELDON PRODUCTION

SPECIALIST EDITOR

Dr Robert W. Boden

TEXT

Dennis Hearne

PHOTOGRAPHY

Leo Meier

MANAGING EDITOR

Kerrie E. Andrews

PRODUCTION MANAGER

Cecille Weldon

DESIGN AND PRODUCTION

John Bull, Bull's Graphics

ILLUSTRATIONS AND FABRIC DESIGN

Isobelle Bruder

ADDITIONAL ILLUSTRATIONS

Yolande Bull

CAPTIONS FOR PHOTOGRAPHS PAGES 1-15

Page 1 Native pear or billygoat plum *(Planchonia careya)* from the Northern Territory.

Pages 2-3 Western Australian flame pea *(Chorizema cordata)*.

Page 5 Fringe lily or fringe 'violet' *(Thysanotus tuberosus)*.

Pages 6-7 Brilliant orange blooms of *Grevillea pteridifolia,* a grevillea of the typical 'toothbrush' type.

Page 8 One of Australia's beautiful orchid species.

Pages 10-11 Delicate blooms of *Murdannia graminea* each last for only one day.

Page 12 Lilly pilly *(Acmena smithii)* blooms.

Pages 14-15 Australian water lily *(Nymphaea gigantea)* of northern Australia.

The Publisher wishes to acknowledge the invaluable assistance of
the staff of the National Botanic Gardens, Canberra and particularly
Mr Ian Telford and Mrs Joan Taylor.

A Kevin Weldon Production

First published 1984 by
Kevin Weldon and Associates Pty Ltd
43 Victoria St, McMahons Point, N.S.W. 2060, Australia
© Copyright Kevin Weldon 1984

National Library of Australia Cataloguing-in-Publication Data

Hearne, D. A. (Dennis A.)
Blooms of the Australian Wilderness.

ISBN 0 949 708 07 0

1. Wild flowers – Australia – Pictorial works.
I. Meier, Leo, 1951- . II. Title.
582. 13'0994

Typeset by Walter Deblaere and Associates, Australia
Printed by Dai Nippon Printing Co. Ltd (Tokyo)

Foreword

*T*HE EXTREME uniformity of the vegetation is the most remarkable feature in the landscape of the greater part of New South Wales, wrote Charles Darwin during his visit to Australia in the summer of 1836. Whilst walking on the sandstone platform near Blackheath in the Blue Mountains west of Sydney he also noted '… the scenery becomes exceedingly monotonous; each side of the road is bordered by scrubby trees of the never-failing Eucalyptus family…' One wonders how different Darwin's impressions would have been had he visited Sydney a few months earlier when the spring flowers which turn the heathland into a riot of colour were in bloom. Unfortunately, many Australians, whether they have lived here all their lives or have arrived only recently, share Darwin's view of the Australian vegetation. They fail to see the subtle changes in tree cover, consisting mainly of eucalypts and acacias, or realise there are over 1300 different species in these two groups alone each with its own distinctive form, leaves, flowers and bark.

We often tend to think how different Australian plants are from those of other countries and this is largely true. Most species occur nowhere else in the world and Australians have a special duty to themselves, their children and people everywhere to ensure that these plants and their habitats are protected.

Blooms of the Australian Wilderness is designed to open our eyes to the beauty and charm of Australian plants but especially those which are less often seen. Through the skilful art of photography the book brings these plants out of the wilderness for all to enjoy. It is hoped that this enjoyment will lead to an increasing awareness of our native plant heritage and concern for its protection.

R. W. Boden, Director, National Botanic Gardens

Contents

Not Just Bush

*T*HE AUSTRALIAN wilderness is at risk. More particularly, vast sections of Australia's irreplaceable flora are not only at risk, but are being actively destroyed on a day to day basis. Unfortunately, the destruction is often not from the action of the multinationals, mining companies or property owners. These easily identified groups undoubtedly cause more than their fair share of destruction in the name of 'progress' but, often are in a position to put things to rights. Not so the less easily identifiable culprits – the huge groundswell group that cause active destruction just by being there. The home owners, rural block dwellers, small farm holders, pasture developers, beach house owners and so on. Each of these groups, passively or actively, is aiding and accelerating the loss of our unique and irreplaceable heritage.

The irony is that, in most cases, these causative agents are in an area because it was, in the beginning, 'unspoilt' or 'natural'. Most rural dwellers immediately clear 'the scrub', put in lawns, hedges of some exotic shrubbery, some 'nice' shade trees and, presto, another evolutionary trend has become an evolutionary dead end. Our native lands contain some of the world's rarest and most beautiful plants, as indicated by A.S. George *et al* in *Flora of Australia* (1981):

The temperate and sub-tropical rainforests of eastern Australia survive today in a number of isolated pockets scattered along the coast

The giants of the rainforest are essential for the maintenance of the ecosystem. Their tall canopies provide protection for smaller, more delicate plants to grow in shaded, moist conditions; their leaf litter decays on the forest floor to enrich the soil and provide a habitat for small creatures. Vines live on the gargantuan trunks and buttressed roots bind the soil.

Growing freely across most of Australia
where water is abundant, the umbrella sedge
(Cyperus alternifolius) bears flower
clusters in striking contrast to the symmetry
of the leaflets.

and ranges, and their total area has been considerably reduced both by logging and by clearing for pastoral activity... They are the surviving residue of the primitive stocks from which the bulk of the modern Australian flora has been derived. This residue... includes some of the most primitive genera of flowering plants still surviving in the world. These are the most ancient Australians still surviving. Perhaps with such an understanding of the history of these forests and with awareness of their intrinsic beauty, we should consider, as a matter of national pride, conserving all that remains of them. The Australian flora, as we see it today, thus tells the story of a hundred million years of history of Australia as a southern land mass...

Blooms of the Australian Wilderness was prepared with an earnest desire to halt the wanton destruction of our native flora and their usually highly specific habitats. In no way does it set out to be a definitive work. Nor does it try to cover our flora in any prescribed, formal manner. Instead, it represents a random collection of plants photographed in various habitats the length and breadth of Australia. The photographs have been chosen for their special features. Some are singularly beautiful, others misshapen and weird. Some will elicit the response of 'oh, that's just a weed; it used to grow in the paddock when I was a kid...' However, crops and weeds introduced from other countries and now naturalised in Australia must legitimately be counted as part of the Australian flora. Unfortunately, they are competing with the natives and creating an instant impact not previously encountered on this continent.

We are Australian people and we should learn to know and love the Australian plants and to appreciate their real values – like their adaptation to some of the harshest and most inhospitable country in the world, their drought hardiness and tolerance to poor and infertile soils. The list is endless. Australian plants have been evolving in response to climatic change and other constraints for millions of years. We cannot ignore them, with scarcely a backward glance, or dismiss them as just so much dull and uninteresting 'bush'.

The genus *Darwinia,* commonly known as the scent myrtles, was named after Erasmus Darwin, grandfather of Charles Darwin. Scent myrtles are extremely variable: some species have 'flowers' (actually petal-like bracts) that hang like little bells; others have flowers in upturned bunches, as in the case of *Darwinia fascicularis,* pictured. An unusual feature of this species is that the blooms commence white then age to a rich cherry red.

Glistening paper daisies *(Helipterum anthemoides),* dot the Victorian Alps with silver tussocks visible for miles, the blooms basking in the brief alpine summer sun.

A delicate symmetry of blooms. The leaves are adapted to harsh environments and a limitless supply of nectar and pollen attracts insects and birds, typifying the numerous *Melaleuca* or paperbark species that inhabit Australia.

A tiny pea flower glows with superb
colour on the forest floor in far North Queensland
near the Daintree River.

Grasses play a vital role in the binding
of soil in the Australian wilderness, especially on
the slopes and plains to the west of the Great
Dividing Range where forested areas become
progressively more sparse. The flowering heads
of grasses are well adapted for later seed
distribution, many having sticky hairs or spikes
that catch on the bodies of animals and birds,
to be transported to a new destination.

ringe lily or fringe 'violet' *(Thysanotus tuberosus)* is a commonly seen perennial throughout mainland Australia but is anything but common in appearance. Each amethyst petal displays a delicate fringe of filaments, seen at their best on a sunny day since, during overcast periods and at night, the flowers close up.

Straw Flower

The straw flowers *(Helichrysum* species)
are one of Australia's most fascinating group of
plants. Members of one of the widespread
and diverse daisy families (Asteraceae), straw
flowers number over one hundred different
species in Australia alone! These species range
in habitat from the humid tropics of the far
north to the windswept heights of Tasmania.
The hard, almost wooden petals and their
ability to close up tightly each night reflect
interesting evolutionary adaptations to a harsh
environment. Small wonder that one of the
common names for this flower is 'everlasting'.
The species *Helichrysum acuminatum* was
photographed in the Bogong National Park
in the Victorian Alps. Scattered in random
profuseness amongst other alpine flora, the straw
flowers provide a brilliant spectacle of molten
gold in an otherwise featureless plateau.

Everlastings beginning to set seed in late summer, here pictured in Ku-ring-gai National Park north of Sydney.

An iris in its simplest form is an
apt description of *Patersonia* which contains
about twenty species native to Australia – only one
has yellow flowers, the rest being various shades
of blue. In bloom, native iris or native flag creates
a beautiful effect: although each blossom lasts only
a few hours, a constant succession of flowers over
a long period maintains the smoky lavender hue
that dots the bushland floor during spring. From
the elegant, three-petalled simplicity of the
blooms are produced russet seed capsules that
open as winter approaches.

Sprengelia incarnata is generally confined
to coastal and coastal mountain habitats in
mainland Australia. The shrub is variable but
usually slender. Terminal flowers, crowded
and surrounded by numerous bracts, make up
showy pink and white flower 'heads'.

A delicate example of the lily family,
Schelhammera multiflora closely resembles its
American cousin, Solomon's seal.

Yellow kapok or wild cotton *(Cochlospermum gillivraei)* is an unusual tropical plant with a haunting, delicate perfume to its pure golden blooms. Leafless for months during the dry season, the plant bursts into glorious colour with the slightest increase in humidity. The fruits that follow begin like green plums then dry and split open to reveal seeds covered in lint that was used by Aboriginals for body and artefact decoration at corroboree time.

The spike, or hair, rushes *(Eleocharis* species)
belong to the same water-loving plant family as the
sedges. Rushes are leafless plants with green stems
and flowering spikes. One Chinese species is
cultivated for its edible white tubers known
as water chestnuts.

One of Australia's few 'carnivorous' plants, the pitcher plant *(Nepenthes mirabilis)* is a wonder of nature. This rambling perennial occupies swamps, mangroves and marshy jungle, using other shrubs for the support of its ungainly canopy. Owing to its saturated environment, typically deficient in nutrients, its leaves modify into 'pitchers' to attract and ensnare unwary insects.

B*rachycome* species are native annual
and perennial daisies. Included in the genus is the
white- to pink-flowered Swan River daisy
(B. iberidifolia) as well as other species with
blue or even purple flowers.

The delicate spider-flowered *Grevillea linearifolia*
has blooms so tiny that they would barely cover a
fifty cent coin. However, in the Ku-ring-gai region
north of Sydney they dot the bush, giving grace
to the straggling shrubs that bear them.

Like prehistoric monsters sunning
themselves on some ancient sand dune, the
leathery, patterned fruit of the exotic melon
remain long after the vine that bore
them has withered and died.

One is inclined to think of the traditional herbaceous daisies or the gaudy sunflowers when the daisy family Asteraceae is mentioned. However, this small alpine bush, *Olearia,* is also in that family. The name *Olearia* is a direct allusion to the similarity of its leaves to those of *Olea,* the olive.

Alpine celery *(Aciphylla glacialis)*
is a stout, tufted plant that does in fact resemble
the celery of kitchen fame. The flattened umbels,
so typical of the Apiaceae family,
are clearly illustrated.

Jacksonia dilatata is a member of the
legume family Fabaceae. From the Northern
Territory, this species hides tiny yellow blooms
amongst masses of bract-like, woolly material.

$\mathcal{S}$undews (*Drosera* species) can be
deceptively attractive to insects that, once alighted
on the 'flypaper' leaves, are digested by the plants'
enzymes to provide supplementary nutrients
deficient in the soil of the sundews' habitat.

In the four legume or pea families there
exist some 12 000 species throughout the world;
their uses to man and nature are innumerable.
The butterfly-like flowers of the Papilionaceae are
extremely beautiful and are characterised by one
large, spreading petal, two wing-like petals and
a keel that contains stamens and ovary. The yellow
markings of the *Hardenbergia* pictured are
a guide to the nectaries for pollinating insects.

The wilderness in close-up: nature has
designed every plant for survival and, in most of
these designs, is an almost unbelievable symmetry
and purpose. White flowers are attractive to
pollinating insects, especially with pretty green
'target' marks. Furthermore, six petals are
matched by six anthers. Floral parts in complex
and consistently recurring threes, fours, fives
and sixes are common in nature and are described
by man through mathematical formulae.

lthough only infrequently in bloom,
the large 'tomato soup' coloured, up-turned bells of
Brachychiton paradoxus, the floral emblem of
Darwin, are spectacular. The wooden capsules that
follow are boat-shaped and contain yellow,
peanut-sized seeds once sought eagerly by
Aboriginals for food. The specific name of this
large shrub refers to the stark contrast of
velvet-like, 'dinner-plate' leaves when young
and the gaunt, black branches, frequently bare
for months, in the mature plant.

Grey spider flower *(Grevillea buxifolia)*
is a delightful small shrub, to about 120 cm in
height, with pretty felt-like stamens tinted
mushroom pink.

lannel flowers are well known to most
eastern Australians. Less famous is the miniature
flannel flower *(Actinotus minor)* which, in almost
all respects except size, is the same as its renowned
relative. The tiny white blooms dot the scrubland
floor but each is smaller than the size of
a one cent piece.

EUCALYPTS

The Australian environment can be one of
the harshest in the world. This fact has provided
some superb examples of plant modification
to cope with external conditions. Not the least
of these modifications can be seen on that
unique Australian tree, the eucalypt or, in the
words of Governor Phillip, the 'gum' tree, which
occurs in various adapted forms in almost all
areas of Australia from the Snowy Mountains
to the semi-arid inland. Species range from
statuesque, graceful trees in open woodlands
and on the plains to stunted mallees in less
ideal conditions, such as alpine areas or the
outback. The very name *Eucalyptus* is derived
from one particularly interesting feature of
adaptation. Coming from two Greek words
meaning literally 'well covered', the name is an
allusion to the mechanism that protects the
developing flower. This mechanism, the
operculum, is a tight fitting seal that grows
as an overall part of the flower bud. Once the
bud is mature and the bloom ready to open,
the operculum lifts off and falls to the ground,
allowing the stamens which serve the dual role
of 'petal' and anther-supporter to expand into
the well-known 'gum blossom'. The mallee
pictured has also evolved another protective
mechanism in its thick, leathery, stemless leaves.
The elimination of leaf stalks and the thickening
of leaves results in a rigid leaf better able to
withstand cutting, sand-laden winds. Other
eucalypt leaves are narrow and hang vertically
from their stems, thus minimising exposure
to the sun's heat and consequent water loss.
Almost all eucalypts shed some
leaves in a dry spell.

Eucalypt seeds form, after the flower has died, in the typical 'gumnut' pods common to most of the species.

The striking two-toned bark of a majestic eucalypt in the Mellong Swamp of Wollemi National Park, New South Wales.

A daisy from the Flinders Ranges in central Australia glistens jewel-like in the early morning. Note the true flowers or disc florets that occur in all daisies, here clearly visible. The surrounding 'petals' are called ray florets.

A bottlebrush (*Callistemon* species) preparing to expose its densely packed stamens to the pollinators that will ensure seed is set.

nce one *Stachytarpheta jamaicensis*
is established in a virgin bush setting, it spreads like
wildfire. The young bushes are compact with
attractive, dark green leaves and the dark blue
flowers, borne on constantly lengthening spikes,
are self-fertile and rapidly produce seeds that
can travel great distances.

The Christmas bell *(Blandfordia grandiflora)*
is one of the best known blooms of Australia.
Its grass-like leaves form tussocks from which
emerge long stalks bearing red and yellow
flowers. The species occurs in moist areas and
may bloom year round although it is in summer
that these exquisite flowers commonly dot
the coastal heathlands.

Prostrate but sometimes climbing,
Oxylobium scandens is a delightful, yellow-flowered
member of the butterfly type pea family
Papilionaceae. With flowers occurring mainly
in spring, the genus to which it belongs is
tolerant of wide habitat conditions and
is well adapted to dry spells.

Legume plants bear bean-like fruit
that browns and dries as it ages. As it splits open,
usually in the heat of summer, the seeds
are released.

A close relative of wandering jew is the delightful little *Commelina cyanea,* at home in tropical marshy areas, creek fringes and other damp locations. The striking blue flowers are produced through all but the coldest months and demonstrate the beautiful symmetry of nature.

The red lotus lily *(Nelumbo nucifera),*
spectacular when seen on a Northern Territory
lagoon. The striking coral pink blooms and leaves
can crowd so tightly together that the water is
scarcely visible. The roots and seeds were
eaten by Aboriginals and this controlled the
proliferation of the plant. Now lotus lilies
are again spreading in appreciable numbers
across northern waterways.

A familiar component of the sand dune
flora throughout Australia, the grass-like leaves of
a *Spinifex* species harbour seed heads designed to
tumble wherever the wind blows them. For this
characteristic they are sometimes incorrectly
referred to as tumble weed.

Handsome, blue-tinged fern-like foliage
more than compensates for the sparse flower
clusters of *Grevillea pectinata,* a spreading
1 m tall shrub from Western Australia.

A tiny *Pseuderanthemum* is dwarfed by
leaf debris on the forest floor in far
North Queensland.

The morning glory family of vines
(Convolvulaceae) is well represented in the
Australian flora and occurs throughout most
habitats from coastal dunes to the harsh, semi-arid
inland. The *Merremia* species pictured occurs
in northern Australia.

$\overline{A}$ustralian hollyhock *(Lavatera plebeia)*
survives only two or three years. However, the
copious seeds that follow the white to mauve,
attractively striped flowers ensure continual
regeneration. It grows to about 2 m.

BEACH HIBISCUS

Beach or Timor hibiscus *(Hibiscus tiliaceous)*
is a hardy, evergreen tree found along the sandy
beaches of northern Australia; it has even
extended its range into the Pacific islands and
much of tropical Asia. Often growing close to
the high tide mark, the tree's litter becomes
a protective home for myriad creatures. Far
reaching, tough and wiry main roots and fine
feeding roots result in the plant playing
an important role in binding sand dunes
and preventing erosion. The blooms of this
beautiful tree are most unusual. Typically
hibiscus in shape, they open a bright, clear,
sulphur yellow and exhibit a striking maroon
eye. On the second day, however, the blooms
turn a rich orange and eventually fall from
the tree. Leaf litter and spent blooms, often
in considerable amounts, collect under the tree
and provide an ideal habitat for hermit crabs
which also devour the fallen blooms.

Beach hibiscus flowers in bloom and the last stage of floral life.

Four-leafed clovers do exist! *Marsilea mutica* belongs to the plant order of ferns and is an oddity amongst its relatives. Growing from the muddy depths of ponds, it sends its leaves up to the water's surface on stems that can be 90 cm long. The spores (by which all ferns reproduce) were reputedly used by Aborigines as a source of flour for small baked cakes.

The Ancient Survivors

J.D. HOOKER, an eminent English botanist, published a book in 1860 that was to set the stage for the next century and provided apparent evidence for the colonisation of the Australian landmass by subsequent invasions of different floras at different times. He was able to show that there was a strong India-oriented representation in the northern Australian flora, Malay rainforest types on the Australian east coast and many New Zealand and temperate South American links with the cool rainforest and alpine floras of southern Australia. These affinities in flora led to the land-bridge theories, which in turn aided the formation of the floating continent theories.

The Indo-Malayan land bridge was thought to have broken up about fifty million years ago, which allowed the flora to develop in isolation. One interesting theory is that the first invading plants came to an Australian landmass sparsely inhabited botanically speaking, so were able to develop under conditions of low competition and subsequently low selective pressures. These reasons have been set up as one possible explanation for the primitive forms of much of the Australian flora. The theory goes on to suggest that Australia's southern (Antarctic) flora arrived in a similar manner and at a time when Antarctica was free of an icecap and extensively populated by temperate climate flora.

*G*aunt and spectacular in bloom, native passionfruit *(Passiflora* species) are widespread throughout the jungles of North Queensland.

Typical of the toothbrush type of floral
arrangement in the genus *Grevillea* is an
undescribed species from the Fitzgerald River
region of south-western Western Australia, with
an affinity to *G. baxteri*. Its pretty red anthers
are a signal for pollinating insects and
honeyeating birds.

The concept of land bridges as a source of plant (and animal) invasions gradually lost credence as more and more specific information on the earth's movements became known. It is accepted fact that earthquakes generally occur in specific linear zones and these zones tend to surround areas that are free of seismic activity. The earthquake-free zones have been called tectonic plates and it is supposed that relative movement between neighbouring plates causes earthquakes along the margin.

The whole of the earth's surface, both on land and under water, can be shown to consist of these plates, all of which are in constant movement relative to each other. In accordance with this movement and by the examinations of similarities and differences in geological structures and in fossilised and existing life forms, it is probable that there once existed a southern super-continent, probably in the Jurassic which ended about 135 million years ago. This super-continent, called Gondwanaland, consisted of South America, Africa, Madagascar, Australia and New Zealand, all clustered around a temperate Antarctica.

Gradually, this land mass broke apart and the continents as we know them came into being. It is thought likely that Antarctica remained joined to Australia for a considerable length of time after this event, possibly through the South Tasman Ridge, and that South America also maintained a tenuous land connection. Both these connections were probably severed in the Oligocene period which ended about twenty-five million years ago. If this latter theory is the correct one for the origins of Australian flora, the implications are staggering.

The basic core of 'ancestor' plants from Gondwanaland are broken into two groups. On one hand, are those that have changed little since geologically ancient times and they are generally inhabitants (or creators) of closed, moist forest cycles. Owing to stability in their environment, there has been relatively little diversification and so definite links with other southern floras can be observed. The other group, mostly temperate and arid-adapted material, shows intense and extreme diversification from the original stock. Usually such plants have small, precisely defined habitats and, often, they exhibit a high resistance to drought and cutting winds, through the presence of a large number of fibres within their structure, obvious leaf and growth habit adaptations and thick cuticles or 'skin'. Paperbarks, bottlebrushes, grevilleas and certain wattles belong to this latter group.

The Simpson Desert, despite its 'desert'
classification, is home to myriad plant species,
including many of the 'poached egg' daisies
(*Myriocephalus* species), so called for the blooms'
deep yellow centres and white surrounds.

Once Gondwanaland split up and Australia went its own way, the flora did the same. Plants adapted and developed characteristics for survival, in accordance with the demands and vagaries of our climate. And the demands are steep. Australia's climate ranges from subarctic to tropical; from rainforests blanketed in cloud to exuberant jungles, subtropical rainforests and deciduous woodlands. Heathlands line the coastal belt and the interior is parched. Every region and every climate encourages individual plant development. Each of these habitats has its own mix of conditions, encouraging some form of life and always plants. Most flower and even those that do not often present their spores or cones in a floral-like manner, contributing to an overall beauty.

Often we take these flowers for granted dismissing them sneeringly and saying 'it's just a bush plant'. But to botanists around the world, Australia's flora is a showcase. More than eighty per cent of our species and almost forty per cent of the genera, are unique.

In each area, plants range from the minute, which need a magnifying glass to view, through to the extravagant giants, often with blooms and colours so vivid they measure up to the most exotic hybrids. Sometimes it does need a hand lens and a willingness to go on hands and knees to discover minute details in blooms. The beauty of Australia's wild flowers is one of our greatest treasures and a distinctive part of our national heritage.

The unusual arrangement of the blooms of this paperbark cause considerable confusion. Unlike most members of the genus, *Melaleuca pulchella* does not produce the typical bottlebrush format. Instead, fused, incurved staminal bundles give a full and fluffy effect giving rise to the common name of claw flower. This weeping shrub, seldom exceeding 1 m in height, occurs in Western Australia.

A tiny ephemeral flower is probably
seldom noticed until the photographer's lens
catches it nestling in dark green leaves
in far North Queensland.

Like wandering jew, its close relative
Murdannia graminea thrives in damp, slightly
marshy places. Often in the company of sedges and
swamp-loving grasses, this little plant has colonised
much of Australia with its glowing, delicate
mauve to pink flowers. The blooms last only one
day but are produced freely throughout
most of the year.

Like fairy lanterns glowing amongst dark
green foliage, the elongated and bell-shaped
blooms of *Correa reflexa* are produced year round
and in profusion. Hardy enough to grow almost
anywhere, including clinging to rocks at seemingly
impossible angles around Sydney's harbourside,
C. reflexa grows to about 2 m.

The black bristle rush *(Chorizandra enodis)* is a hardy and attractive sedge that occurs throughout most of Australia's southern States where it may be seen growing at the edge of bogs or still water.

J ewelled and glistening, the sundews
(Drosera species) offer as pretty a trap as could
be found for unwary insects. The leaves of drosera
terminate in soft spines, each covered with
a sticky secretion. This acts both as a 'flypaper'
trap and allows digestive enzymes to break down
the soft portions of the trapped body. In this
way the plant supplements impoverished soil
with essential nutrients and is thus able to
occupy ecological niches not heavily contested.

Looking so much like a bottlebrush
that mistakes are often made when identifying
this bloom in the bush, *Melaleuca elliptica* makes
a compact, 2 m shrub that displays its brush
flowers, often up to 8 cm long, to perfection.
Deep red is just one of the colours displayed by
paperbarks, others being cream, yellow, orange,
mauve and crimson. Botanically, paperbark blooms
are distinguishable by their bunched stamens,
here clearly evident.

Net bushes or one-sided bottlebrushes
(Calothamnus) consist of about twenty-five
species. Their delicate, wax-like and textured
'petals' are actually bunches of
stamens, similar to the related bottlebrushes but
occurring only on one side of the stem.

The dandelion is so common throughout
Australia that it rarely attracts a second glance.
However, since arrival in Australia from its native
South Africa, the large and spectacular clumps of
attractive blooms have been seeding prolifically
to invade native scrub throughout the
temperate zone.

The golden garland lily *(Calostemma luteum)*
thrives in bright sunlight on the banks of
inland rivers in South Australia, New South Wales
and southern Queensland.

Seen in extreme close-up, the true flower
of the kangaroo paw (*Anigozanthos* species) is
apparent. The unusual floral structure actually
consists of a comb-like arrangement of hairy
bracts from which emerge the fused petals
of the blooms, creating the likeness that
the common name describes.

ORCHIDS

Australia possesses an enormous
wealth of orchids with some seven hundred
species of ground-dwelling (terrestrial),
rock-clinging (lithophytic) and tree-dwelling
(epipthytic) types. Those that cling to rocks and
trees are best known and easily spotted, but
conscientious searching in open woodlands
and forests can reap the reward of a delicate
terrestrial peeping out to expose its blooms.
Dendrobium striolatum, pictured, grows on
granite boulders along watercourses, the golden
flowers making a superb display against the
sombre colouring of leaves and rocks. The
terrestrials tend to occur in southern temperate
and far northern areas with distinct high and
low rainfall seasons while epiphytes need a
fairly constant supply of moisture and therefore
are most common in tropical and subtropical
rainforests. Although relatively recently evolved
orchids are amongst the most diverse of plant
groups in the Australian flora. However, no
proven fossil records of orchids have yet been
found. All native orchids, many of them rare,
are protected plants.

The tall sun orchid (Thelymitra media) *favours valleys in undulating forest as well as low lying flats in heavily, forested areas. Far more widespread than T. ixioides, this species occurs in all States, including Tasmania.*

Commonly called donkey or double tail orchids, Diuris species are almost totally confined to Australia. Only one species is endemic to Timor, while more than forty other species range over temperate Australia. D. aurea ranges from the Atherton Tableland in Queensland to south of Port Jackson in New South Wales.

The name Thelymitra *comes from the two Greek words* thelys, *'feminine' and* mitra, *'a headdress', an apt description of the hair tuft that decorates the column of the members of this genus. This magnificant colour form of the dotted sun orchid (T. ixioides) typifies the species, but colours may range through to pale mauve and almost white. It occurs in temperate regions of all the States.*

Bejewelled with dew drops and shimmering like some rare treasure, the large wax lip orchid (Glossodia major) was amongst the earliest of the Australian orchids named. Described by Robert Brown in 1810, the generic name Glossodia *refers to the 'forked tongue' appendage between the column and labellum. It occurs in all States except Western Australia and the Northern Territory.*

A colour variant of Lyperanthus suaveolens, *one of four species of the rare orchid genus* Lyperanthus *that occur in Australia in both dry heathland and swampy, sandy habitats. The spring flowers have a vanilla perfume; species often flower profusely only after bushfires.*

Called the lawyer orchid, presumably owing to its association with the calamus palms or 'lawyer vines', Sarchochilus olivaceus does have many other hosts, including trees, rocks and rotting stumps. The blooms are highly fragrant and are produced during the dry season in northern Queensland.

Pink fingers is an apt common name for Caladenia carnea. One of the most heavily perfumed of the Australian native orchids, it gives off strong, musk-like scent at night.

The bearded orchid (Calochilus campestris) is one of the beauties of the Australian orchid world. This small terrestrial produces only one leaf each year – an insignificant effort until the richly bearded yellow-green blooms emerge from the single flowering stem.

A Sydney rock lily (Dendobrium speciosum) *presents a beautiful summer display with long, dense clusters of cream to yellow flowers.*

Hyacinth orchid (Dipodium punctatum) *is a well-known and spectacular component in open woodlands, from coastal Northern Territory to New South Wales. The orchid is leafless and usually found in association with eucalyptus trees on which it was once thought to be parasitic. It is now known to be a saprophyte, living on dead organic material.*

The chosen site of this Sydney rock lily (Dendrobium speciosum) typifies the hardiness of the plant. Preferring the exposed Hawkesbury sandstone in the Sydney region, this rock-dweller can stand periods of extreme dryness in summer but nevertheless produces a dazzling display of pale yellow blooms on spikes up to 50 cm long.

Looking like some belligerent insect rearing up to devour its prey, this delicate greenhood orchid is widespread through montane Victoria and Tasmania, but is seldom abundant.

Attractive golden pea-shaped flowers
hide the poisonous attributes of a number of the
'rattle pod' annuals and perennials (*Crotalaria*
species), widespread throughout Australia.
The inflated seed pods, which rattle like a maraca
when shaken, are actually poisonous to stock.

minute, beautiful yet hardy groundcover (*Frankenia* species) of the Fitzgerald River region of south-western Western Australia. With small stem-clasping leaves, modified into miniature water storage tanks, it is ideally adapted to thrive in its dry-baked environment.

The pine-leafed geebung *(Persoonia pinifolia)* is a handsome plant with pendulous branches; often it reaches a height of 4 m. Terminal clusters of sulphur yellow blooms followed by bunches of grape-like fruit have made this shrub of the Australian east coast a favourite of florists and gardeners.

Ornamental and popular with birds,
red five corners *(Styphelia tubiflora)* once grew in
abundance around the first settlement of Port
Jackson and so captured the settlers' imagination
that it was stocked by English nurseries from
the beginning of the nineteenth century.

Guinea flowers *(Hibbertia species)*
are versatile scrambling plants. Equally at home on
coastal sand dunes and the floors of moist, open
forest on the Australian east coast, *Hibbertia
scandens* has long, woody, trailing stems and
pretty, bright yellow flowers.

S*ida corrugata* is a prostrate undershrub
that develops trailing stems up to 60 cm long.
Pale yellow blooms develop irregularly throughout
the year and are up to 3 cm in diameter. The plant
thrives in the drier parts of all mainland States.

SPIDER FLOWER

Grevillea is a diverse genus of over
250 species and many more hybrids, both natural
and man-made. The genus was named after one
of the founders of the Royal Horticultural Society
of Great Britain, Sir Charles Greville. Specimens
in this group can range from the impressive
silky oak tree *(Grevillea robusta)* to some of our
smallest bushland plants only centimetres
high. Many of the smaller types are actually
prostrate or semi-prostrate groundcovers.
Grevilleas occur all over the continent, from
Tasmania to the farthest northern shores,
from east coast to west. In general, grevillea
flowers are quite distinctive, but the
arrangement of the blooms is as varied as
the foliage in this beautiful genus. One-sided
'toothbrush' type spikes are common in the
eastern States, as are the more symmetrical
'spider' type clusters of blooms. In the tropics,
arrangements like a candelabra and even
pendulous 'bottlebrush' types are common.

Once the early morning sun illuminates the floor of Wollemi National Park, New South Wales, the true beauty of the blooms of the wilderness is apparent. Glistening with dew, a cluster of tiny pea flowers sparkle like amethysts in nature's garden.

The blood water tree and fish killer tree
are only two of the common names for *Barringtonia
acutangula*. In the wild, the tree overhangs creeks
and billabongs which become covered with its
dying, blood red flowers. In a good year, the
flowers, produced in great skeins, turn the water
quite red. The allusion to fish killing is derived
from the old Aboriginal ploy of dumping the
tree's crushed, leafy branches into water, thereby
introducing a chemical that suffocates fish and
causes them to float to the surface for
easy collection.

I t would be unfair to call the royal poinciana *(Delonix regia)* a weed. However, it is becoming a serious competitor with Australian flora. Glorious in flower, when the entire leafless crown becomes a brilliant scarlet, it produces hundreds of seeds. Trees mature extremely quickly and provide dense shade, precluding smaller native plant growth.

eset with a halo of soft hairs to
deter predatory insects, the purity of shape and
colour in the blooms of the Australian wilderness
is obvious when viewed in close-up.

On tropical beaches, such as those that
occur on Hinchinbrook Island in North Queensland,
Cordia subcordata is a common plant identifiable by its striking orange, crinkly blooms,
heart-shaped leaves and walnut-sized,
cork-wrapped seeds.

M osses and liverworts reproduce by
spores – each an asexual, microscopic single cell
– which, when distributed, grow into an organism
with both male and female sex cells that, after
fusion, produces a baby plant. Here the spore
cases of a moss assume a military appearance.

Poetry in motion as miniature white blossoms
pause momentarily amongst jungle stream flotsam
in the Daintree River region of far
North Queensland.

Honey myrtles or paperbarks (*Melaleuca* species) make up a widespread group of some 140 species of shrubs and small trees, most of which have white, papery bark that was used by Aboriginals to make watertight baskets and even canoes. Paperbarks occur throughout most of the country but many prefer damp, poorly drained soils. The nectar-laden flowers range from ivory to red and appear in spring and summer. *M. nesophila* has beautiful mauve-pink flowers and stem-clasping leaves. Leaves of other species range from oval and fleshy through to fine and needle-like, depending on species and habitat.

133

Love-in-the-mist or stinking passionfruit
(*Passiflora foetida*) is an introduced plant in
northern Australia where it is both destructive and
dangerous. The strongly flavoured fruit is edible
and popular among native animals; however it is
both the growth habit, which tends to smother
any plant it uses for support, and the lush green
leaves' resin which bursts into a hot blaze
in the presence of fire, that contribute
to the destruction of the native flora.

Saw Banksia

Saw banksia *(Banksia serrata)* is a grand old
patriarch of the Australian bush in the eastern
States; it usually develops into a spreading,
10 m shrub with branches so gnarled and twisted
that it appears to be positively ancient.
The large flower spikes are spectacular and much
sought by florists for their size and grey-yellow
tonings. However, it is the seed cones that follow
the blooms that will live on in the memories
of most Australians. These cones were the
models from which the 'big, bad banksia men'
of Snugglepot and Cuddlepie fame were drawn.
With their numerous gaping 'mouths' –
actually the follicles from which the seeds
have been expressed – these innocent, though
bizarre seed cones must have frightened
generations of Australian children.

one flowers (*Isopogon* species) are most unusual small shrubs of the protea family. With over thirty species, occurring mostly in Western Australia but also in other mainland States, these hardy plants bear densely packed, globular flowering heads of yellow or pink and generally pretty, divided leaves. The species well known in the New South Wales bush is named drumsticks (*I. anemonifolius*) and here demonstrates the aptness of its label.

Many fungi are useful in helping to break down organic material, releasing nutrients into the soil for healthy plant growth. Here, one of the shelf, or bracket, fungi is hard at work reducing a fallen branch into available plant food.

Symbolic of the complete circle that nature
follows, the skeletal remains of a dead leaf rest
against the vibrant green of sphagnum moss plants.
Decayed leaves provide nutrients for the moss
which provides a fibrous soil in which leafy
plants thrive. The plants' leaves drop and
the cycle repeats.

Native Plants in Close-up

THE FLORA of the Australian wilderness is generally equated with just a few of the 15 000 or so species that occur in this country and, most specifically, with eucalypts and wattles. With almost 1500 species between them, they are justifiably our two most important plant groups, for reasons of both economy and beauty. As national 'identities', however, they must share the stage with a few other plants – those that have been selected as floral emblems and that have, as a result, heightened people's awareness of the beauty of our native plants.

EUCALYPTS

Contrary to popular belief, *Eucalyptus* is not the largest Australian plant genus, but it is the most significant. In fact, its members dominate ninety-five per cent of our forested areas. It is estimated that there are between five hundred and six hundred distinct species and all but a few are Australian. Of the nine species that occur outside Australia, only three are endemic to their regions.

Eucalypts generally occur in open forest or woodland groups but exhibit little adaptation to rainforest or alpine situations, although some species do occur in these locales. The species are immensely variable and many attempts have been made to classify them into sub-groups. Indeed, some authorities think it possible to reclassify *Eucalyptus* into nine groups.

Early morning light shines through
a stand of *Melaleuca leucadendron* paperbarks
in Kakadu National Park, Northern Territory.

Of the eucalypts, the silver-leafed ironbark
(Eucalyptus shirleyi) is not typical of the genus but is
nevertheless a magnificent asset to Queensland's
Atherton Tableland. The broad, stem-clasping
foliage is extremely glaucous in both the juvenile
and adult stages and forms a perfect foil for
the large clusters of cream blossom.

For largely practical reasons, this sort of classification has never been completed but practical sub-divisions based on field observations have become common. Thus it is quite correct to lump plants together as 'bloodwoods', 'ironbarks', 'stringybarks', 'peppermints', 'ashes' and 'gums'.

Eucalypts in general show a long association with fire and indeed contribute significantly to the flammability of the Australian bush. This long association has led to numerous adaptations to the fire regime. Many species have thick, woody, insulating bark, which does not support burning. Others develop large numbers of subcortical buds which provide rapid shoot and branch regeneration after fires. Many others develop large, woody ligno-tubers which act as reservoirs in dry times as well as providing unscorchable bases from which new plants can regenerate, even if all above ground growth is lost. Other eucalypts have not specialised to save themselves; instead, they have developed woody seed capsules which only open to release seeds after a fire has scorched them.

The extreme flammability of eucalypts is thought to be a defence mechanism in itself. The presence of so much volatile oil in eucalyptus leaves ensures a very rapid burn, which quickly destroys all easily consumed fuel and allows a rapid return to normal temperatures. This prevents the destruction of dormant buds, which would be damaged if exposed to a cooler, slow-burning, all-consuming fire.

Eucalypts have been cut and harvested by white men since we first came to these shores. Many species yield valuable hardwood timbers. Other uses include the manufacture of paper pulp, cabinet making and utilisation as bridge pylons. The leaves of many species are distilled to yield valuable oils used in pharmacy, perfumes and, frequently, industrial applications. Still other species provide tannin from the bark. Possibly the best known products, however, are famous honeys such as blue gum and yellow box.

WATTLES

The other enormously successful plant genus in Australia is *Acacia,* the wattles. Australia's unofficial national floral emblem is *Acacia pycnantha,* the golden wattle, and our official international sporting colours are the green and gold — a direct reference to wattle. Despite the highly popular nature of the wattle, the genus is still not fully understood. The name

The delicate pom-poms that make up the
familiar globular flowers of Australia's wattles
(*Acacia* species).

'wattle' was first applied by Australian colonists to a totally unrelated shrub, *Callicoma serratifolia,* used in the construction of the settlers' 'wattle and daub' huts. The transference of name from *C. serratifolia* to *Acacia* no doubt came about through the similarity of flowers, the callicoma having cream cluster flowers that resemble those of acacias.

Nowadays, there are at least 800 recognised species in the *Acacia* genus, making it the largest in Australia. Few of them yield valuable products and so, unlike the eucalypts, many species have escaped the axe. *Acacia* is also well represented in the floras of Africa and tropical America but, there, most species tend to retain normal foliage. In Australia, just one section – the Phyllodinae – dominates the representation and in this section, true leaves are reduced to an enlarged leaf stalk, often flattened, which then functions in the manner of a leaf. This feature is generally regarded as an adaptation to arid conditions.

Acacias have a greater range over the Australian wilderness than even the eucalypts and frequently form a large percentage of many separate ecosystems. In this respect it is interesting that over forty per cent of *Acacia* species occur in the south-west of Western Australia. The beauty of *Acacia* flowers is known world wide. Flower clusters may vary in colour from pure white to golden orange and from the characteristic fluffy balls to long and pendulous or rigid and upright clusters.

FLORAL EMBLEMS

Floral emblems are an official recognition by the States of a native plant for one reason or another. Sometimes this plant may be representative of the State's flora but more often it merely grows particulaly well, or perhaps is threatened, in its home land. Whatever the reason, however, the creation of official floral emblems is one way to immortalise blooms and to make the general public more aware of them. One State, the Northern Territory, has gone so far as to include a representation of its emblem, Sturt's desert rose *(Gossypium sturtianum),* in the official State flag. A classic lesson in the looseness of common names, Sturt's desert rose is neither confined to the desert nor is it a rose. Instead, it is first cousin to the cotton of commerce and a near relative of the popular garden hibiscus. A shrubby, often sprawling, low plant with thick, leathery blue-green leaves, the desert rose grows in clay pans and deep sands,

S turt's desert pea *(Clianthus formosus)*
is the official State floral emblem of South Australia.

rocky slopes and road verges. Delicate lavender-blue flowers with a prominent red eye are borne freely throughout most of the year.

Western Australia has chosen a striking bloom for its emblem. Brilliant emerald green and strident fire-engine red should scream at each other when brought too close together but, in the kangaroo paw *(Anigozanthos manglesii)*, the colours meld into a superb flower arrangement. One of nine species of kangaroo paw, this plant is under investigation in cancer screening tests in the United States. Blooms are borne on long spikes, well clear of the reed-like foliage. The unusual floral arrangement is well adapted to pollination by honey-eating birds.

South Australia has, without doubt, the most spectacular flower of all for its floral emblem. This time the common name is more accurate; Sturt's desert pea does in fact occur naturally in the desert and is indeed a member of the pea family. That the naming authorities were impressed by the beauty of this plant is obvious in their choice of the generic name *Clianthus.* This word comes from the Greek 'kleos' meaning glory and 'anthos' meaning flower. *C. formosus* is indeed a 'glory flower' as it spreads in random riot over dunes, creating mats of blue-grey foliage that displays to perfection the brilliant red and black of the flowers.

Queensland chose for its emblem the Cooktown orchid. This lovely native plant is notoriously variable in form, colour and growth, leading in the past to confusion. Some authorities have referred to the species as *Dendrobium phaleanopsis* which, although extensively cultivated here, is not an Australian native. The correct name for the Cooktown orchid is *Dendrobium bigibbum.* While never approaching the Sturt pea for brazen display, the long arching spikes of lavender to pink blooms are charming and beautiful. The species has figured widely in hybridising programs and imparts a dwarfing feature to pseudobulbs and usually a rich colour to the blooms.

With so much heathland in Victoria, the perfect choice for the floral emblem was one of the native heaths – in this case, *Epacris impressa,* the common heath. It grows to a height of around one metre, less than half that of other species in the family, and the long, narrow leaves (often only 6mm wide) are prickly. Unlike other members of the family, the common heath does not flower the year round, restricting its display to winter when tubular red, pink or white blooms are arranged densely along the tips of the stems. The name *Epacris* is misleading for the common heath: it means 'on a mountain', for this is where the first members

S tanding proud and regal despite its
advancing age, the waratah *(Telopea speciosissima)*
is New South Wales' floral emblem. Waratahs,
which belong to the same family as grevilleas
and banksias, have long been grown by gardeners
for their exquisitely beautiful flowers.

of the genus were found. This species is not found above 1000 m, growing most commonly on lower mountain slopes and coastal heathlands.

New South Wales' emblem needs no special introductions, as its brilliant blazing red waratah *(Telopea speciosissima)* is justly famous worldwide. The Aboriginal name of waratah was adopted for the plant in the early stages of European settlement; both Aboriginal legends and European botanists and artists have been inspired by this bloom. *Telopea,* from the Greek word 'telopas', means 'seen from afar' and, certainly, during spring time, the glowing red coals of the waratah blooms can be seen from great distances. *T. speciosissima* is not the only species of waratah. Three species exist in the wilderness and several man-made hybrids are grown in gardens.

Tasmania chose one of the forest giants for its floral emblem. The Tasmanian blue gum *(Eucalyptus globulus)* can make a massive tree of 60 m or more in height and develop trunks over 2 m in diameter. This species was extensively planted in a number of overseas countries during the early nineteenth century – so much so, in fact, that in India, New Zealand, California and Italy, it is now regarded as native! In some areas of India, notably the Nilgiri Hills, the species has exceeded 80 m in height. Similarly, in Italy the tree is one of the major aids being used in draining the infamous Pontine marshes. Producer of honey, of invaluable hardwood, of distinctive blue foliage, *Eucalyptus globulus,* beloved of florists, is really an all-round beauty of the Australian wilderness.

The Australian Capital Territory also has a floral emblem – the royal bluebell *(Wahlenbergia gloriosa).* At most a tuft-forming plant, this alpine beauty occurs only above 1300 m in the mountains from New South Wales to Victoria. Abundant in the Australian Capital Territory, royal bluebells exhibit rich purple, star-like blooms in spring and summer.

In both bloom and fruit, the rainforest fringe tree known as *Dillenia alata* is a beautiful sight. In stark contrast to the lush green foliage, large sulphur yellow blooms are followed by dramatic capsules filled with brown seeds covered with white flesh. When the pods burst open to eject the seeds they look like red flowers. The empty capsules remain on the tree, as beautiful in the last stage of the floral life cycle as in the first.

Lechenaultias are delightful little shrubs
from Western Australia; some have incredibly rich
blue flowers but others are red, yellow or even
cream. Here, an extreme variation in form is seen
in the almost pure white, heavily ruffled petals of
Lechenaultia species from the arid
centre of the country.

Tawny bronze berries set off by
leathery, dark green leaves typify the pepper
creeper *(Piper caninum)* of Queensland
rainforests. Its Indian relative, the common pepper,
bears fruit which is ground to make the
familiar spice.

Old man's beard, as our native species
of the beautiful group of *Clematis* climbing plants
are called, is often more spectacular in
fruit than blossom.

espite having over a hundred recorded
species, the plants of the genus *Goodenia* often pass
unnoticed. Growth habits can vary from tiny
shrubs scarcely 3 cm high to much larger, spreading
or erect plants. The species pictured is a scrambling
groundcover from the Simpson Desert.

One of the worst of Australia's introduced
plants is caltrop or puncture weed *(Tribulis astoides)*
which competes with a number of native *Tribulus*
species, all of which produce a spined burr.
Superbly adapted to coastal and desert areas,
tribulus has some use in erosion control. Yellow
blooms quickly set many seeds, resulting
in massive proliferation.

revillea rosmarinifolia is a variable plant.
Its narrow, pine-like leaves and stiff branches form
a dense shrub to about 2 m tall and the same wide.
It blooms throughout most of the year but,
although both colourful and beautiful, this
spider-type grevillea's flowers are often
obscured by the thick foliage.

For several hundred kilometres south
of Darwin, the large, brilliant orange blooms
of *Grevillea pteridifolia* glow in the bushland.
This 'toothbrush' type grevillea has silvery,
fern-like foliage.

A spider-like flower cluster typifies
Grevillea capitellata, a highly variable but beautiful
shrub of the New South Wales scrublands.

MANGROVES

Mangroves comprise one of the most important, single components of the Australian flora. Apart from the obvious protection they provide for large tracts of the island continent's shoreline, mangrove communities are essential for much of the country's coastal food chain system. They support other plants, such as epiphytic orchids, provide cover for various crustaceans and, for birds, an ideal source of marine and insect food. In addition, mangroves themselves are uniquely adapted to be the only woody plants capable of withstanding continuing tidal salt inundation. Leaves expel salt drawn up through the roots; 'cobblers peg' roots, bizarre and stilt-like, are specially developed to obtain oxygen from the air and seeds, with the ballistic skill of a wartime bomber, are specially weighted to bury themselves right way up in mud or sand. Seeds can also float for long periods and, in some species, the young plant has even sprouted from the seed before dropping from the parent tree.

Amazing root formations created by the mangroves of Hinchinbrook Island, Queensland.

Young mangroves establish themselves on the tidal flats situated on the leeward side of Hinchinbrook Island.

A new mangrove emerges from its staff-like seed case,
firmly embedded in the tidal mud.

A perfect example of the root system developed by certain mangroves. It ensures a firm roothold, as well as allowing the tree to withstand salt water inundation.

*M*elastoma affine is a variable shrub that flowers almost continuously in tropical Australia. The generic name comes from the Greek words meaning 'black mouth', owing to the stain incurred from indulging in too much of the delicious 'blackberry jam' pulp that surrounds the dust-like seeds.

Like tassles of silk, the unusual flowers of
she-oaks *(Casuarina* species) briefly beautify
the dull grey-green, needle-like foliage of a tree bent
on survival in a harsh environment.

Lilly pilly trees *(Acmena smithii)* need little introduction in east coast Australia for there they make beautiful garden subjects. The fluffy, cream blooms nestle in small clusters amongst glossy green leaves and are followed by large and striking, purple edible berries.

Despite the tendency of *Grevillea
tripartita* to flower less than many of its better
known relatives, it displays a singular beauty
on close inspection. Rigid, prickly leaves
protect the delicate red and yellow blooms and
are also an efficient adaptation in the face of
its often dry environment in Western Australia.

The thickly massed fruit of a jungle fig
(*Ficus* species) provide an essential food base
for insects, birds and other animals and,
in the past, even man.

Flax lilies (*Dianella* species) range from
the tropical north to the coldest parts of Tasmania.
The blue flowers are followed by equally
brilliant purple to blue berries.

A nodding blue lily *(Stypandra glauca)*
which occurs throughout Australia with strap-like
leaves and bright blue flowers. The delicate,
pendulous flower clusters and prominent anthers
make nodding blue lily an excellent example of
the beauty of our native lily family species.

PLECTRANTHUS SUAVEOLENS

A pungent mint smell drifting up from
the forest floor reveals the presence of *Plectranthus
suaveolens,* a member of the mint family.
The slightest touch on one of the soft, fleshy,
hairy leaves releases a deliciously spicy odour.
When the actual plant is located, the exquisite
beauty of its small spikes of bluebottle-like
flowers is apparent. Rich mauve spotting deep
in the throat of the flower acts as a
'runway signal' to guide foraging pollinators
to the hidden nectaries. In following these
signals to their banquet, the pollinators, be they
fly, bee or moth, cause the fertilisation of the
flower. Four *Plectranthus* species occur in
Australia, all of them with the aromatic
properties that contribute to the famous,
much-loved perfume of the Australian bush.

Tea trees (*Leptospermum* species) acquired
their common name from the old method of eking
out dwindling tea supplies by adding the leaves of
several species. The delicate flowers are borne
in profusion in winter, spring and summer, their
fine, white to pink petals brightening the shrubs
and trees and attracting bees and birds.

Brightly painted 'landing strips'
on a shrub from the Fitzgerald River area of
Western Australia provide clearly visible markings
for pollinating insects.

The velvety bloom of the exquisite flannel
flower *(Actinotus helianthi)*, is almost too perfect
to be real. The down-covered plant often grows
happily in the poorest of soils, sometimes
finding roothold in little more than a patch
of sandstone gravel.

The family Fabaceae, the legume-bearing plants with distinct pea-shaped flowers, is well represented throughout Australia. Although plant and leaf forms run the full gamut of variability, the basic flower shape remains the same. *Pultenaea,* with over a hundred species, is the largest genus of endemic Australian pea flowers and produces dense terminal heads of usually yellow or red blooms.

The purple, elongated, edible fruit of the
giant pigface *(Carpobrotus glaucescens)* is one of
Australia's most delicious wild fruits. The plant
is a natural resident of sand dunes, colonising
the coastal dunes before most other vegetation.
Blooms, of the typical pigface type, occur
throughout the year and are most numerous
in spring and summer.

Every niche in the Australian bush
supports plant growth perfectly adapted for that
area. The delicate groundcover *Cassia aciphylla*
is no exception. In the sub-tropics of eastern
Australia it carpets slopes and forest floors with
bright green leaves and pretty,
bell-like yellow flowers.

Aboriginals of northern Australia prized
the fruits of the cockatoo apple, otherwise known
as native pear or billygoat plum *(Planchonia careya)*.
The spectacular and graceful blooms that
precede the fruit, although regrettably short-lived,
are a common sight during the build-up to
the wet season in the tropical north.

DARLING LILY

One of the most spectacular sights that
can assail the lucky bushwalker is the discovery
of a colony of Darling lilies. In southern areas
the species *Crinum flaccidum* (pictured) is most
common; in the far north it is *C. indicum* and
C. uniflorum. The beauty provided by this group
of plants is without peer: crystal-pure, gleaming
white, newly opened blooms and the heavy,
sweet perfume so typical of the genus constantly
delight the senses. The perfume attracts a wide
variety of insects, so the absence of bees in some
areas of the Darling lilies' range is of little
importance. All insects are welcome to the
copious nectar – in drinking deep they transfer
pollen and thus ensure future generations of one
of our most spectacular blooms. Undisturbed
areas of the country may boast hundreds or even
thousands of these beautiful plants which, in
flower, transform drab, half-dried swamps
into elegant gardens.

The daisy families are well represented
in Australia with some hundred different groups.
The daisy bloom is actually composed of hundreds
of tiny flowers clustered in a circle and surrounded
by showy, petal-like ray florets. The fibrous-rooted
daisies, such as the species pictured, are known
as Asteraceae and occur the length and breadth of
the country. The *Brachycome* illustrated
is a classic example of the beauty of daisies.

Mulla mulla, silvertale or, more
correctly, *Ptilotus,* is a widespread genus of over
a hundred species. At their best in the semi-arid
Northern Territory they occur, however,
in all mainland States.

The name of the genus *Scaevola* means
'left-handed' since most species develop a lopsided
flower. Despite their unusual lack of symmetry,
these are common plants that occur along most
of the Australian coastline and are extremely
salt-tolerant.

The perennial gentians, with the
well-known blue flowers, occur in cool climate
areas on all continents and islands such as
New Zealand and Japan. In the Victorian Alps,
however, thrives a mauve-striped, white
gentian *(Gentianella diemensis)* with the
characteristic funnel-shaped blooms
of the genus.

Wax flowers *(Eriostemon* species), of which there are some thirty-two species, are delightful drought-tolerant, low-growing shrubs that bear pink to white blooms. Pink wax flower *(E. australasius)* has a temperature tolerance of 0° – 35°C.

Wonga wonga vine or monkey flower
(Pandorea pandorana) is one of Australia's
spectacular creepers. Although extremely variable
in both flower colour and leaf form, all the varieties
bloom profusely. The purple-spotted throat
is a guide for pollinating insects.

One of our most beautiful violets,
no less attractive for its abundance in damp areas
from far North Queensland to Tasmania, is the
ivy-leafed violet *(Viola hederacea)*.

Man-Friend or Foe?

*T*HE PHYSICAL act of mining, the disturbance of an ecosystem, the infiltration of roadways through scrub lands and the spillage of wastes, both toxic and non-toxic, have all contributed to massive destruction of our wilderness areas in the past. Indeed, in the Northern Territory, at the site of one of the early uranium mines, there is still an area totally bare of all plant growth. The area was not destroyed by radiation but by spillage of toxic chemicals used to extract metals from the crushed ore. A broken tree skeleton – gaunt, stark reminder of the scrubland that once flourished there – bears mute witness to man's indecent haste.

Fifty years of nature's leaching has done little to rehabilitate the site, but man has done nothing at all. Fortunately, such devastation is rare in the region. Nearby, at the rural town of Batchelor, a huge open cut mine has become an artificial lake, full of fish and aquatic creatures. Intelligent planting and landscaping are transforming the barren overburden into a delightful park – not the original bushland, nor anything like the original, but it does represent an earnest attempt to correct the depredation of a previous era.

Nowadays, mining companies are putting botanists and horticulturists into the field, before beginning operations, to give the companies an accurate picture of the plants that exist, what ratio they have to each other in the community and what association they have formed. The

The rainforests of tropical Queensland
form a verdant, lush and complex ecosystem where
all elements of life are linked to each other.
When one part of the chain is broken, the entire
rainforest can be threatened.

In the Daintree River region of north Queensland the rainforest's canopy of myriad designs protects the lush environment.

companies collate this information before the inevitable destruction of plant life that accompanies mining operations. Seed collections, nursery establishment and plant propagation are becoming an integral part of mining. In this way, the unique flora of an area is not destroyed irrevocably.

On the New South Wales coast, revegetation of plants following sand mining for rutile and other valuable minerals has been an outstanding success. Dunes had weathered to such a degree that hinterland vegetation had begun to suffer from salt-laden winds, so horticulturists visited the area, collected seeds, took cuttings, lifted bulbs and, in short, did everything possible to collect from the very plants threatened by the mining operations. Nursery activities were started and it is recorded fact that information gained in this phase of the operation has assisted nurserymen throughout Australia to propagate hard-to-raise native plant material. Botanists performed population counts, made careful analyses of ratios of one species to another and prepared to recreate the bushland once mining operations were completed. Topographers, aware of dune deterioration, calculated the original height and contours of the dunes.

After the miners had moved in and areas of coast had been torn apart as giant machines extracted the valuable minerals and disgorged the unwanted sand, other machines rolled in and recreated the dunes. The only thing missing was a mineral probably dispensable to plants. When reshaping and recreation of the dunes was completed, replanting was commenced. The end result is 'virgin' bushland ablaze with colour provided by the natural vegetation of the site. As at the New South Wales rutile site, replanted areas frequently surpass undisturbed surroundings, because of a redistribution of nutrients in the soil. The plants show healthier growth, more vigour and brighter colours. Most of all, they become more reproductive and help, in fact, to reclaim those areas damaged by other causes.

Significantly, the outstanding triumph of the New South Wales project has set a standard for all mining operations. Profitability of an operation now must be such that natural revegetation can be undertaken. It is no longer sufficient to grass over an area or put some forest trees onto a mined site. All mining sites in the Northern Territory have resident horticulturists on staff and most have stringent regulations restricting non-native plants being replanted in the area. One such site, the Jabiru uranium mine area, even limits the flora to those species native only to the Jabiru region.

If the miners have shown the way, the property owners have been quick to follow. In a welcome upsurge of awareness, graziers in marginal lands are replanting the native scrub. For example, the much-slandered Murray mallee has been found to have an invaluable role in the ecology of the plains of the interior. Originally it was chopped out mercilessly, regarded as fit only for firewood. Crops were planted and, in good years, provided reasonable yields; but in the bad years when drought dominated, wind erosion quickly scoured out the delicate soil, leaving only clay and limestone flats where nothing could grow. Some farmers have turned back to the mallee, planting thousands of young plants. Once established, they rehabilitate the plains, providing cover and shelter for the ephemerals – those small shrubs and delicate annual and perennial wildflowers that typify so much of the marginal lands of Australia.

Not only the mining operations and the croplands are gaining from rehabilitation. Shifting sand dunes, land slides, eroded fields and contaminated flood plains are all benefiting from revegetation. Our native plants, evolved over millions of years to handle the vagaries of Australia's climate, are gaining a new role in Australia's industrial and agricultural progress and also have attracted interest overseas. The deserts of Saudi Arabia, Israel and the Gulf States are turning green with eucalypts, wattles and saltbush. The eucalypts and wattles change the micro-climate and spinifex settles shifting sand dunes by anchoring them with its spreading roots and sprawling branches.

In India and some Caribbean Islands, eucalypts are solving a fuel crisis. Desperate for an energy source, some countries have adopted the eucalypt to replace their own depleted forests – forests composed of slow-growing and unprofitable species compared to some of our tropical eucalypts that produce a 5 m tall tree in a single year and can yield enough wood for charcoal or firewood in only two or three years.

Around the world there is a growing awareness of the strengths and benefits of our native plants. In world terms, it is a tiny recognition, limited by the restricted availability of our native plants and the lack of international knowledge about them. Even so, a handful of countries have seized upon them. In California, the aroma of profusely growing eucalypts, wattles, paperbarks and bottlebrushes fill the air and remind one of the Australian bush. San Francisco has even adopted for its floral emblem the Western Australian red flowering gum, *Eucalyptus ficifolia*.

Nothing is ever wasted in nature's garden.
Detritus from the forest breaks down to help
provide the ideal environment for mosses and ferns
to develop from microscopic spores into the minute
'prothallus' (sexual) stage, from which grows
the mature plant. Leaf and twig humus collects
in damp, rocky cracks – an ideal niche
for a young fern.

Daintree, in far north Queensland,
is one of the last areas of Australia where rainforest
wilderness survives to meet the coastline.

A clump of native iris (*Patersonia*
species) brightens a precipitous rocky outcrop
overlooking the Colo River gorge in
New South Wales.

Others have been adopted for their beauty alone. In the Lakes District of England, en route to Windemere, is a magnificent old garden; a rockery covering many hectares. One of the biggest trees there, and one of the healthiest examples of the species this writer has seen, is *Eucalyptus gunnii,* a Tasmanian expatriot holding pride of place in the beautiful setting, happily thriving in a misty, cool garden on the other side of the world.

In yet another area, it would seem that our beautiful and precious native flora are being elevated to the status they deserve, for Australia has been highly active in recent years in declaring National Parks. Sometimes these parks are protected by legislation that has teeth but, all too often, the park becomes another bit of land, set aside now but destined to be nibbled away by vested interests as the years pass. The prime idea behind any National Park is to set aside an area of specific importance. Such an area might house a rare or near-extinct animal or plant. Perhaps it contains weird, bizarre, monumental or just plain beautiful physical features. Whatever the reason, land set aside as National Parks should be kept in its pristine glory forever – and most people would agree with this philosophy. However, the irony is that preserved land, simply because it is preserved, is immediately under attack. Roads are constructed, providing perfect entry ways for plant disease, weed invaders and human litter. Physical amenity blocks discharge their wastes into fragile ecosystems. Mining, when allowed, disturbs the area and, of course, farm or feral animals all play their part.

The recent drought disaster of 1982-1983 in the Mt Bogong region of Victoria resulted in starving cattle being turned loose into the National Park. The emergency measure was used in several drought-stricken areas and, faced with the short term decision, it was probably the correct one. Farmers' losses were minimised, cattle lived instead of starving to death and no one could argue that these were not positive results. However, within weeks of the drought breaking, weed invaders were everywhere in Bogong National Park. The new plants with short life cycles reproduced so rapidly that they quickly overwhelmed that natural vegetation with limited reproductive cycles. Herbaceous plants that had never been grazed were unable to compete with better adapted weed species and so succumbed without a fight. Similarly, bushes stripped of their foliage by starving beasts were unable to store sufficient food supplies for the brutal cold season. The result was death and destruction of a vital part of the unique Australian alpine ecosystem.

Prickly pear *(Opuntia* species) once was
virtually eradicated from vast areas of central
Queensland by the introduction of the cochineal
bug. However, prickly pear again invades warm
areas of eastern Australia, probably inadvertently
encouraged by man since the fruit is delicious
but the seeds germinate easily.

Again, in Victoria, it is the coastal swamplands that are at risk, even though they play a vital part in the overall food chain. In Queensland it is a colony of rare bats. In the Northern Territory, Kakadu trembles before the onslaught of tourist busses, cattle, feral pigs and buffalo. Western Australians similarly see the beginnings of the end, as great karri trees that have lived since the time of Julius Caesar fall prey to *Phytophthora cinnamomi,* an insidious imported fungus. The preventative measures of prohibiting vehicles from travelling through infected areas is, to a large extent, a case of too little, too late.

Often, destruction is accomplished by the simplest things. The heathlands of South Australia and Western Australia are not producing seed for new generations of plants and the culprit is the imported honey bee which, unable to rob many of our plants' specialised nectaries, has taken to chewing into the bloom in search of its liquid treasure. Bypassing normal pollination methods and, at the same time, taking the attractant for natural pollinators, the bee is effectively killing off a number of plant species. Furthermore, being aggressive and better able to survive around settled areas where man makes water available, it displaces native insects. Thus plants more amenable to bee pollination produce more seed than normal and the result is further imbalance in an ecosystem already seriously threatened.

If a National Park is meant to be representative of the untouched wilderness, then how can it – a living thing – be kept in stasis? How can we view and appreciate this vanishing Australia without destroying it as we watch? The parks cannot be frozen in time yet neither can we allow them to become so changed in character that they no longer reflect the reasons for which they were preserved. Australians must face this complex problem in the near future if the children of 2000 A.D. are to know and appreciate the blooms of the Australian wilderness.

In the cool of early morning at the onset of the wet season, Kakadu National Park takes on a brooding appearance. This wilderness of Arnhem Land is renowned for the huge variety of habitats enclosed in its confines, from rainforest to tree-dotted plains punctuated with rock escarpments.

Grass-like plants that colonise swamps
and slow-flowing stream edges, *Lomandra* species
have ornamental, razor-edged leaves that stand
in contrast to the intricate flower structure.

The family Fabaceae (from the Latin *faba*,
'a bean'), is widespread throughout Australia
and contains many of our most beautiful trees
and shrubs including *Gompholobium*.

Caesalpinnia mimosoides is a delicate
northern Australian herbaceous perennial that
provides ephemeral beauty on disturbed land
in the early wet season.

One of the papilionaceous or butterfly-
flower legumes, here illustrating the floral form
common to all the Fabaceae family.

The pretty yellow-flowered *Lindsayomyrtus brachyandrus* tree is rare in its habitat of the Daintree River region of far north Queensland. The tree's range is thought to have once extended from New Guinea through to Mossman in north Queensland but now it occurs only in isolated pockets that could disappear if the rainforest is further threatened.

WALLUM BOTTLEBRUSH

The bottlebrushes *(Callistemon* species)
are splendid and well known native plants.
At least twenty-five recognised species and
innumerable cultivars exist; many hybrids and
cultivars are so prolific in flower that they
virtually hide all foliage on the plant. The name
'callistemon' is derived from two Greek words
meaning 'most beautiful' and 'stemon', an
indication not only of their visual appeal
but also of the form the flowers take. Bottlebrushes are composed of individually free
stamens, unlike melaleucas and others whose
stamens are joined into bunches. Most
bottlebrush blooms are laden with nectar to
attract pollinating insects and honeyeating
birds. Wallum bottlebrush *(C. pachyphyllus),*
pictured, is a shrub to about 1.5 m high
and the same wide. Flower colour can vary from
red to burgundy and even to green. Seed capsules
create their own beautiful patterns along the
stems of the plant; often three or four years
of produced capsules may remain on a
branch at one time.

Alpine mint *(Prostanthera cuneata)*
is a delightful plant, equally at home at low or
high elevations in the montane regions of Victoria
New South Wales and Tasmania. At higher
elevations it is low growing, prostrate or rock
hugging. Lower elevations generally produce
a plant around 35 cm tall. The delicate pattern
of purple and yellow dots in the throat of the
bloom provides perfect 'runway signals' for
any would-be pollinator.

One of the most beautiful of the forty
or so species of *Pimelea* is the rich rose of
P. ferruginea from the coastal region between Perth
and Albany, Western Australia. The flowers, which
last several weeks on the shrubs, can range
from green-tinted white through cream
and yellow to red.

In far North Queensland on Cape York
Peninsula is Mt Tozer, home of a recently
discovered but as yet un-named *Baeckea* shrub.
Its beautiful and prolific fine-petalled blooms
of white, pink and green ensure that this
heath myrtle will ultimately become one
of the well known beauties of the
Australian wilderness.

Brilliant gold in frothy waves,
an exciting and spicy-sweet perfume and delicate,
lacy foliage all add to the beauty of *Cassia
cdorata,* from Queensland and New South Wales.

Appropriately called dagger hakea or dagger bush, *Hakea teretifolias* is well able to protect itse f against foraging animals by forming dense and spiny thickets in New South Wales, Victoria and Tasmania. The delicate cream blooms nest e amongst the needle-tipped foliage.

Like some succulent strawberry
in long, glistening clusters, this bushland fruit
is set to attract fruit-eating animals that will
distribute the seeds.

A hardy little plant distributed throughout eastern Australia, New Zealand and Papua New Guinea, *Achaena anserinifolia* and its relative, sheep's burr *(A. ovina),* form seed heads which, when dry, cling to sheep fleeces and hook into animals' fur as an effective form of seed distribution. The leaves of *A. anserinifolia* also make an acceptable tea substitute.

Simpler in form and yet in many aspects
more beautiful than its commonly cultivated
relative, the native gardenia *(Gardenia megasperma)*
has large, sweetly scented blooms that perfume
the bushland of the Top End.

The cape or crested wattle *(Albizia lophantha)* comes originally from Western Australia but may also be seen growing quite happily in natural conditions in the eastern States. The yellow-green spikes of flowers have a peculiar smell but the physical beauty of both blooms and leaves is a match for this large shrub's close relatives, the wattles.

The lush tropical growth of the Atherton
Tableland behind Cairns includes a large number of
native gingers such as *Alpinia coerulea* var. *rubra*.
This red-leafed ginger has terminal clusters of
vibrant blue berries that develop after the
sweetly perfumed flowers.

Related to the humble carrot and celery, *Platysace lanceolata* is a compact, variable shrub that, in season, may be totally covered with clusters of tiny white blooms.

ACACIA UNCINATA

Surely no other plant symbolises Australia
like wattle. Best known of all our native flora,
wattle *(Acacia* species) actually began life
misnamed. It seems that the name 'wattle'
originally applied to a plant named *Callicoma
serratifolia,* a tall shrub with pom-pom like cream
flower clusters but totally unrelated to the
wattles. This plant was the preferred component
of the wattle and daub construction of the early
settlers. Gradually the name 'wattle' or 'black
wattle' became the accepted name for *Callicoma*
and, over a period of time, became applied to
Acacia, no doubt through the similarity of the
flowers. History aside, one of the most striking
and long-flowering wattles is the species
A. uncinata, pictured. An often straggly shrub
with pendulous branches and brilliant golden
blooms, it flowers over most of the year.
Blue foliage provides the perfect colour
foil for the blossoms.

Native rosemary *(Westringia* species) has
dark green rosemary-like leaves and delicate white
to mauve flowers most prolifically borne in spring
and summer. The shrubs grow from the windy,
salt-laden coast to the coldest mountain areas,
depending on species, all exhibiting a hardiness
unusual even for many native plants.

The hardy, spreading shrub called coastal rosemary *(Westringia fruticosa)* grows in some of the toughest country in New South Wales, including along the windswept south coast. Belying its hardiness are the tiny, delicate purple-spotted blooms that cluster around the tips of the branches.

As if to prove its frozen origins,
the Australian version of the well known New
Zealand veronicas is a symphony in tonings of blue.
Disc-like, blue-grey foliage on supple, spreading
branches and spikes of mauve-blue flowers all
suggest the origin of *Parahebe perfoliata* –
protected places at high altitudes in New South
Wales and Victoria where winters are long
and summers are cool.

Boronia is a genus of some seventy species
and contains some of our most sweetly perfumed
and pretty plants. The famous brown boronia
(B. megastigma) is popular with gardeners and
florists for its magnificent scent. Illustrated is
Sydney boronia *(B. ledifolia)* which, although
lacking the penetrating aroma of that species, more
than compensates with its masses of flowers
and intense pink colour.

Red hot pokers, tulips and hyacinths
known exotic plants of the lily family
(Liliaceae). Less well known is the fact that
Australia is home to several beautiful lilies;
among them Christmas bells, Gymaea lily
and this exquisite species with gracefully
arching white petals.

One of the scrambling morning glory species,
Ipomoea pes-caprae plays a vital role in the binding
of sand dunes in the Northern Territory.
The spectacular blooms are held clear of bright
green leaves which, with rapidly spreading and
snaking stems, provide an ideal habitat for
many foreshore creatures.

Growing exuberantly on the lee of sand
dunes on Northern Territory beaches is the blue-
leafed, blue-flowered groundcover *Vitex ovata*
(syn. *Vitex trifoliata* var. *ovata*). There it is
vital in maintaining dune stability.

With a brilliant display of yellow
and orange, pea-shaped flowers in spring, *Pultenea
stipularis* grows as an erect shrub to about 1 m
in its native New South Wales.

Cootamundra wattle *(Acacia baileyana)*
is one of the most common and best-loved of
all wattles. Its silver-blue leaves, great clusters of
golden bloom in July and August and extremely
handsome shape have resulted in its spread,
by man, and naturalisation, in many parts
of Australia beyond its native New South Wales.

Trigger plants (*Stylidium* species) are
well adapted for pollination. As insects penetrate
blooms in search of nectar, they set off the hair
trigger reaction of the column, which snaps
down to strike the intruder smartly on the body,
exploding the ripe anthers and depositing pollen.
Job temporarily done, the trigger then re-sets
itself for the next visitor.

Sea celery is an appropriate name for
Apium prostratum which occurs in coastal regions
of southern Australia and New Zealand. A single
plant may ramble and spread to create a mat
several metres across, over rocks and ground
alike. Debris left by natural dying back in older
patches provides an ideal nursery bed for less
hardy and vigorous plants.

HEATH BANKSIA

Banksias are truly superb native plants
with their often brilliantly coloured flower cones
rearing proudly above foliage or hiding
demurely behind tough, generally grey-green
leaves that range from long, narrow and spiky
to broad and serrated. The genus *Banksia*
was named in honour of Sir Joseph Banks,
the botanist who accompanied Captain Cook in
the *Endeavour* on its first voyage of exploration.
Heath banksia *(Banksia ericifolia)* is a strikingly
handsome plant displaying cylindrical, erect
flower spikes, up to 35 cm long, well clear
of the foliage. The flowers range in colour
from orange-red to bronze, often seeming like
little flames in the midst of a mass of bushland
greens and greys throughout coastal New South
Wales. The specific name of *ericifolia* alludes
to the fact that the finer, spiky leaves of some
of the forms resemble the native heaths
of the *Erica* genus.

Cooktown orchid *(Dendrobium bigibbum)*
is the floral emblem of Queensland.

Everlastings or paper daisies *(Helichrysum bracteatum)* bear their multi-coloured, large flower heads in spring and summer.

The elegant native crinum 'lily' *(Crinum pedunculatum)* thrives in far north Queensland, where this specimen was photographed, and along the east coast of Australia to Port Macquarie in New South Wales. The star-like clusters of white blooms and the delicate tracery of long pink stamens have made the native crinum popular with Australian gardeners.

Crowea saligna, one of a small group of
fragrant, evergreen shrubs, occurs between the
coast and the mountains in eastern Australia.
On heathlands and sandstone plateaux,
its delightful star-shaped, pink to mauve
flowers dot the shrub.

The soft, deeply divided foliage of
Geranium solander and its delicate pink flowers may
not much resemble the well known exotic
geranium but the native geranium is equally
hardy amongst tree roots, on stream banks
or rocky cliff faces.

South American deadly nightshade has
relatives the world over, from the ubiquitous
tomato and potato to several Central Australian
desert species. In many cases the plants are armed
with needle-sharp spikes which often contribute
to the plant's overall attractiveness.

Showing considerable promise for
sand dune stabilisation is the vigorous creeper
Canavalia maritima. It can cover an area several
metres square in less than one year and its
attractive spikes of bright pink, pea-like flowers are
produced throughout summer. Aboriginals ate the
bean-like seeds, contained in woody pods
that ripen in autumn.

Dried and spent but nevertheless still beautiful
are the seed capsules of a native hibiscus.

*I*T TOOK photographer Leo Meier six expeditions and more than two years travelling to capture his blooms of the Australian wilderness. From the snow-blanketed alps to the steamy tropical rainforests and mangrove swamps of the Northern Territory. Over heathlands and wading through coastal swamps. He remembers it all with affection.

"There is an incredible range and depth to Australia's native blooms... from fragile tropical flowers that seem too frail to survive a day to twisted old plants clinging stubbornly to a barren sand dune. The wonderful devices nature has given these plants to survive in such a varied and harsh environment is part of their fascination."

All photographs in this book were taken with Nikon cameras on Kodachrome 25 and 64 films.